Western Apache woman harvesting an agave plant.
Photograph taken in 1906 by Edward S. Curtis (Smithsonian Institution #76-4665).

INDIAN USES OF DESERT PLANTS

BY JAMES W. CORNETT

Cover photograph:
Dolores Patencio, a Cahuilla woman
of the Sonoran Desert, grinding seeds
in a bottomless basket affixed to a rock mortar.
Photograph taken in 1932.

Cover background photograph:
Mesquite pods.

Facing title page photograph:
Prickly Pear Cactus, *Opuntia engelmannii*.

Opposite page photograph:
Pima woman winnowing mesquite beans.
Photograph courtesy California Historical Society,
Department of Special Collections,
University of Southern California Library.

Unless otherwise noted, photographs are by the author.

Enlarged and updated third edition.
Copyright 2011 by James W. Cornett.
All rights reserved.

Published by
nature trails press
P.O. Box 846
Palm Springs, California 92263
Telephone (760) 320-2664
Fax (760) 320-6182

International Standard Book Number (ISBN): 978-0-937794-45-6

CONTENTS

Desert agave, Agave deserti, *near*
Anza-Borrego Desert State Park, California.

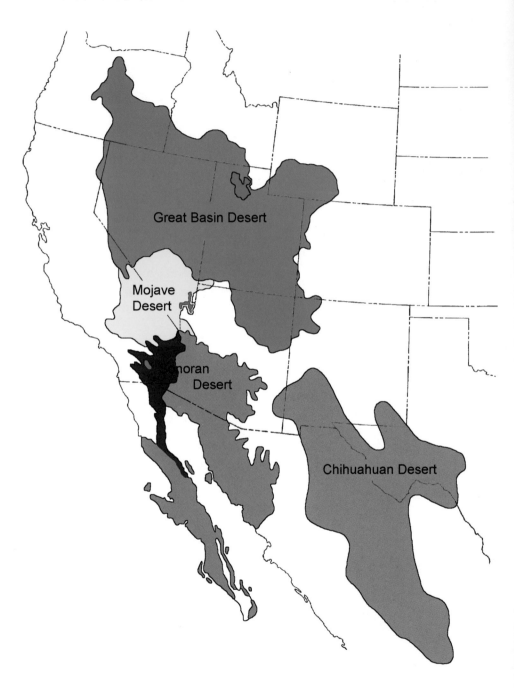

Great Basin Desert

Mojave Desert

noran Desert

Chihuahuan Desert

NORTH AMERICAN DESERTS

Introduction

Deserts of the Southwest contain a multitude of plant species that have sustained human life for thousands of years. Plants provided most food resources as well as raw materials for medicines, tools, shelter, and ceremonial objects. American Indians discovered Jimson weed provided relief from pain, leaves of the desert fan palm could be made into a waterproof roof, and blossoms of the ocotillo provided a pleasant snack. Indeed, knowledge held by Indians regarding their botanical environment was, by necessity, vast.

Native Americans were not simply gatherers of fruits, seeds, and other resources provided by wild plants. Every cultural group used various techniques to store and preserve food plants, often for periods lasting several months or even longer. Some tribes practiced various forms of agriculture—from simple scattering of seeds at sites of likely germination to intensive irrigation and modification of desert landscapes. Many groups were known to carefully select seeds from the best stock to improve yield, taste and nutrition of future crops. All this transpired long before Europeans arrived in America.

One of the often overlooked aspects of harvesting food resources in hunting and gathering societies is the contribution of women. For decades academic and popular literature portrayed men as important, if not the primary suppliers of food for the family and village. Yet numerous recent studies have shown that in hunting and gathering economies women provide the bulk of food resources through collecting of leaves, roots, fruits, and seeds—often more than ninety percent of all food consumed! There is every reason to believe this was the case with most Indian groups living in the desert regions of North America.

Today, commercial agricultural products have replaced native plants in Indian diets. Valuable information regarding desert plants, that passed from one generation to the next, is no longer necessary to sustain life and in danger of being lost. As society moves onward, it risks leaving behind the often untold knowledge of the desert's first people.

Much evidence suggests reclaiming Indian plant knowledge could benefit humans in many ways. Who would guess, for example, that delicious wine can be made from organ pipe cactus fruit, creosote bush may hold the secret of dissolving kidney stones, or gourds might reduce the growth rate of malignant tumors in humans.

In this expanded third edition I have selected 22 plants, or groups of related species, that were of special significance to desert Indians prior to A.D. 1800 and before extensive contact with Europeans. Though not all tribes used each species in the same way, I have attempted to glean from the literature and interviews with Indian consultants practices that seemed of general occurrence. If a use was specific to a particular cultural group it is stated in the text. Plant groups or species are arranged in alphabetical order by common name.

In the writing of this book I have relied, for the most part, on the knowledge and research of others. The efforts of many of these individuals are reflected in the references section at the end of this book. Several Native American persons provided information and insight into the ways Indians interacted with the desert's botanical environment. For sharing their special knowledge (and patience with my ignorance), I am deeply grateful to Native Americans Katherine Saubel, Ernest Siva, William Campbell, and Dora Prieto. Anthropologists Manfred Knaak and Harry Quinn examined the manuscript for technical accuracy. My wife, Terry Cornett, reviewed the manuscript to improve the clarity of my thoughts. Sincere appreciation is extended to each of these individuals.

Zuni waffle gardens used to grow traditional crops of melon, herbs, and chilies. Photograph circa 1915. Museum of New Mexico, Santa Fe.

11

AGAVE
(Genus *Agave*)

Agaves were one of the most important plant groups. Not only did they provide both food and fiber, agave products were valuable trade items because not all villages had access to the plants. Only yuccas, due to greater numbers and an extensive geographic range, were more important.

After cooking, most parts of the agave could be eaten including the leaves, flower stalks, blossoms, and seeds. The flower stalks were harvested in spring and summer. Leaves were juiciest from November to May and provided fresh food when other resources were unavailable.

Agave harvesting required strength and for many tribes it was a male activity. In some areas hundreds of stalks were gathered in a single day. It is not an exaggeration to say that a man's worth was determined, in part, by his ability to find, harvest, and properly cook agave leaves and stalks. Leaves were collected by prying the entire plant out of the soil. Both the leaves and stalks were roasted in large pits to be eaten or pounded into cakes and dried in the sun for later consumption. The leaf mass was eaten like a giant artichoke and, when the charred outer leaves were discarded, a brown juicy mass was revealed that tasted like molasses.

Agave flowers were boiled to remove bitterness and could either be eaten immediately or sundried. If not harvested, flowers produced seeds that were gathered and ground into flour. Some Apache Indian groups removed juice from young flower stalks to make an intoxicating drink known as pulque. (Distilled, pulque is the main ingredient of tequila.)

Agave fibers were used to make bowstrings, brushes, cradles, nets, shoes, skirts, mats, rope, baskets, and snares. Leaves were soaked and pounded to release the fibers which were dried and separated by combing.

Eight species of agave occur in the Southwest and all are characterized by succulent, spine-tipped leaves and a single, towering flower stalk. Agaves are found on coarse soils below 5,000 feet in elevation. Their range extends from the Great Basin Desert of Utah south into Mexico.

Lechuguilla, Agave lechuguilla, *with flower stalk,*
Carlsbad Caverns National Park, New Mexico.

Agave roasting pit site.

Red Rock Canyon, National Conservation Area, Las Vegas, Nevada.

BARREL CACTUS
(Genus *Ferocactus*)

A barrel cactus is commonly thought to have a juicy interior that can provide a life-saving drink of water. Yet evaluation of the liquid from the California barrel cactus, *Ferocactus cylindraceus*, indicates it is too alkaline to drink. Indeed a person would be worse off after drinking the liquid, not to mention the water lost through perspiration while attempting to break open the tough exterior!

Seri Indians of the Sonoran Desert were aware eating the juicy pulp of barrel cactus did not provide life-giving moisture. They have recounted how the juice from the California barrel cactus and Coville barrel cactus (*Ferocactus covillei*) was not considered potable and that it caused headaches. The juice from the fishhook barrel cactus, *Ferocactus wislizenii*, often caused diarrhea and pain in the extremities.

The barrel cacti did provide food. All products of the plant's reproductive cycle were consumed providing a harvest that lasted several months. Women collected the buds and flowers in spring and fruits in early summer. Plant parts were plucked from the top of the cactus with two sticks to avoid the sharp spines. They were then parboiled to remove bitterness. After cooking, all parts were eaten or dried in the sun for storage.

There were other, though less important, uses of barrel cacti. The cactus body was of sufficient strength and size to allow it to be used as a container by cutting off the top and digging out the interior. The seeds were collected, crushed, and mixed with water to make gruel. A medicinal use was to remove the spines from a slice of cactus, roast it, then wrap it in cloth and press it against sore places on the body to relieve pain.

A barrel cactus is characterized by a cylindrical shape and vertical rows of curved spines. Height varies from two to ten feet. Flowers can be yellow, orange, or red, depending upon the species, and form a ring on the top of the stem. Barrel cacti can be found on alluvial plains and hillsides below 6,000 feet in the Mojave, Sonoran, and Chihuahuan deserts.

California barrel cactus,
Ferocactus cylindraceus,
Indian Canyons Tribal Park, California.

Beavertail cactus in bloom, Mojave National Preserve, California.

Beavertail Cactus

(Opuntia basilaris)

Cacti, particularly those species with flattened stems or "joints," were important food plants for Indians living in the deserts of the American Southwest. The beavertail cactus, *Opuntia basilaris*, was one of the most important species in this group because of its predictable occurrence, very small spines, and relatively large yield of fruit.

All above-ground portions of the plant were consumed. The stems or "joints," were broken off the main plant with a stick and rubbed in the sand to remove tiny spines called *glochids*. The joint were then cut into small pieces, boiled in water and either eaten as greens or mixed with other foods. The Panamint Indians of Death Valley dried and stored the joints as well as the flower buds for later use. When needed, joints and buds would be boiled with a bit of salt and eaten.

In spring, up to six flowers emerge from the top edge of a joint. It is possible to have scores of joints per plant. Thus, a single beavertail can produce a great deal of fruit, most of which ripens and becomes very sweet by summer. Collecting was accomplished by knocking the fruit from the joints with a stick, brushing off the glochids with a handful of grass and placing the fruits in baskets. At camp, the fruits were buried in an earthen pit with many hot stones and cooked (or steamed) for up to twelve hours. Upon removal from the pit, they were eaten or stored for later use.

The beavertail cactus contains rather large seeds within its fruit. These seeds were sometimes removed, ground into a meal and mixed with water to make an edible mush.

There were some medicinal uses of beavertail. To reduce pain and aid the healing of cuts and wounds, a dressing was made with the fleshy pads. Pulp would be scraped from a joint and placed directly on the wound. This dressing was changed several times each day.

Glochids were sometimes rubbed into moles and warts in the belief such a treatment would remove them.

Beavertail cactus can be identified by its low, spreading growth and flattened pads that are bluish-green or lavender in color. There are no noticeable spines. The large pink or magenta flowers appear in spring.

Individual plants are most often found on coarse-soiled alluvial plains and hillsides below 6,500 feet. The beavertail's range includes the desert regions of California, southern Nevada, southwestern Utah, southwest Arizona and the Sonoran Desert of Mexico.

Close relatives of the beavertail are the prickly pear cacti also in the genus *Opuntia*. Native Americans ate the young joints as well as the reddish fruits. At least one species of prickly pear is found in each of the four North American deserts.

Fruits and pads of the prickly pear cactus, Opuntia engelmannii, *Saguaro National Park, Arizona.*

Cocopa woman of the Sonoran Desert grinding seeds, Smithsonian Institution photograph circa 1900.

COTTONWOOD
(Genus *Populus*)

Female cottonwood trees produce thousands of seeds covered with long, white hairs. Wind captures the hairs, carrying the seeds over vast distances. Often seeds are blown against a fence or dwelling where they may form feathery piles several feet deep. The origin of the common name "cottonwood" comes from the cottony fruits consisting of the hairs plus seeds.

There are about forty species in the genus *Populus*, the genus to which cottonwoods belong. All species require permanent or nearly permanent moist soil in which to grow. For this reason desert species are associated with streams, rivers, springs or seeps. Fremont's cottonwood (*Populus fremontii*) and narrow-leaved cottonwood (*Populus angustifolia*) are the species most associated with the Southwest.

When available, most Indian groups used the cottonwood's large forked branches as the framework for houses and ramadas. The bottom of a branch was buried in the ground and the erected fork provided support for beams. Beams were either large cottonwood branches or wood from other trees such as willows (*Salix* spp.). The dead and dried branches of cottonwoods made excellent firewood.

Several early ethnobotanists wrote how the wood was used to make tools. However, the only specific tool for which a literature citation could be found appears in Lowell Bean and Katherine Saubel's book *Temalpakh*. Bean and Saubel describe how a short section of cottonwood trunk would be cut and the top hollowed out. The result was a cottonwood mortar used to grind fruits and seeds of such plants as mesquite. The technique avoided the pitfall of rock mortars that resulted in tiny, abrasive rock fragments in the ground substance.

Cottonwoods also had medical applications. Skin or epidermal inflammations or infections could be bandaged with a poultice made of the damp cottony fibers attached to cottonwood seeds. Boiled leaves and bark poultices were also used for this same purpose.

Cottonwood tree in fall,
Canyon de Chelly, Chinle, Arizona.

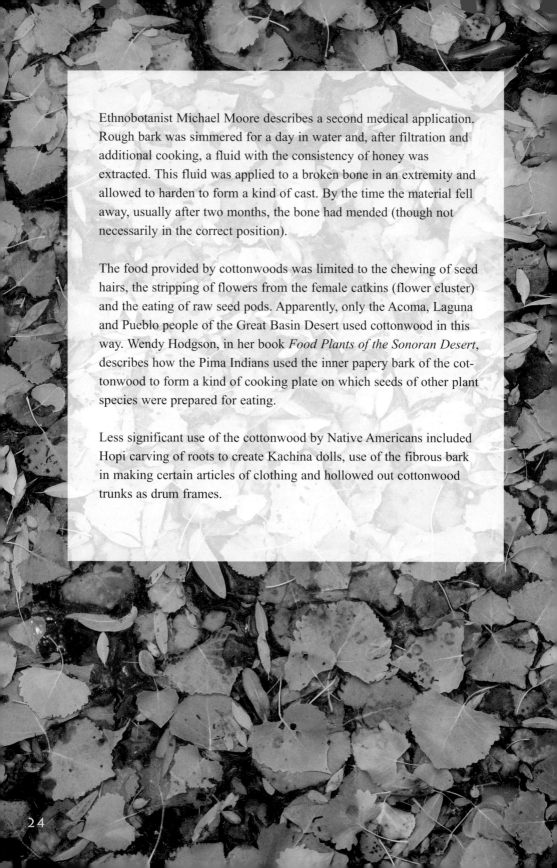

Ethnobotanist Michael Moore describes a second medical application. Rough bark was simmered for a day in water and, after filtration and additional cooking, a fluid with the consistency of honey was extracted. This fluid was applied to a broken bone in an extremity and allowed to harden to form a kind of cast. By the time the material fell away, usually after two months, the bone had mended (though not necessarily in the correct position).

The food provided by cottonwoods was limited to the chewing of seed hairs, the stripping of flowers from the female catkins (flower cluster) and the eating of raw seed pods. Apparently, only the Acoma, Laguna and Pueblo people of the Great Basin Desert used cottonwood in this way. Wendy Hodgson, in her book *Food Plants of the Sonoran Desert*, describes how the Pima Indians used the inner papery bark of the cot-tonwood to form a kind of cooking plate on which seeds of other plant species were prepared for eating.

Less significant use of the cottonwood by Native Americans included Hopi carving of roots to create Kachina dolls, use of the fibrous bark in making certain articles of clothing and hollowed out cottonwood trunks as drum frames.

Chapa Alamo, a Cahuilla Indian, grinding seeds in a cottonwood mortar (circa 1910).

CREOSOTE BUSH
(*Larrea tridentata*)

The creosote bush is the most widespread perennial in the deserts of North America. From Death Valley in California to Big Bend National Park in West Texas, this shrub reigns supreme. Given its vast range and abundance, it is not surprising creosote is one of the most important food plants for desert animals. Less realized is its historical importance for American Indians living in the Southwest.

The strong scent of the creosote bush foretells the unusual chemical composition of its foliage and hints at its medicinal value. South-western Indian tribes used the creosote bush in as many ways as modern medical practitioners use antibiotics. In fact it was a veritable medicine chest! A dry powder made from the leaves was discovered to be an effective antibacterial agent when applied to cuts, abrasions and burns. The pain of rheumatism and sciatica was reduced when the afflicted area was rubbed with a compound of crushed creosote stems and water. Indians with tuberculosis were given a drink made from leaves and stems boiled in water. This *tea* (though nearly undrinkable) was said to cure simple respiratory infections, constipation and cramps associated with delayed menstruation. Some Indian groups used the tea to treat venereal diseases.

As a remedy for respiratory problems, the Cahuilla Indians would inhale vapors produced from boiling leaves in the confines of a structure known as the sweathouse. If the house was not available, the patient (while covered with a blanket) would inhale from a vessel of steaming creosote vapors.

An important chemical compound in creosote leaves is called nordihydroguaiaretic acid (NDGA). In one clinical study this substance was shown to inhibit the growth of cancerous tumors in laboratory animals. Unfortunately, a second study suggested that the substance appeared to accelerate the growth of tumors. Future studies will shed more light on the value of NDGA in cancer research.

Creosote bush dominates a
Chihuahuan Desert landscape in West Texas.

Although the medicinal value of creosote bush was premier, there were other categories of use. Flavors of certain foods were enhanced by cooking over a creosote wood fire. The resin-like exudate of an insect known as the lac scale was collected from the surface of creosote branches and used to mend pottery and waterproof baskets.

The creosote bush grows from three to twelve feet high. It can be identified by its small, yellowish-green leaves and dime-sized, yellow, five-petaled flowers. When pollinated, the flower ovary matures into a small, fuzzy white fruit. Over vast areas of the Mojave, Sonoran, and Chihuahuan deserts the creosote bush is the most common perennial plant on well-drained flatlands and hillsides.

Creosote flowers, hair-covered fruits, and leaves,
Montezuma Castle National Monument, Arizona.

DESERT FAN PALM
(*Washingtonia filifera*)

The only native palm in the western United States provided a rich abundance of material resources for the Indians of the Sonoran Desert. Categories of utility included food, construction material, tools, clothing, weapons, ceremonial objects and, of course, shade.

The fan-shaped leaves of the fan palm are remarkably long-lasting. With knowledge of this durability, Indians pulled the leaves from trunks and used them to thatch roofs and walls of their dwellings.

Palm fibers were used to make baskets, although they did not wear as well as those made from the stems of *Juncus* or sumac. Sandals were commonly manufactured from palm leaf fibers and were still worn as footwear when writer George Wharton James visited the Cahuilla Indians in the late 1800s. Palm leaf stems were carved into shovels, spoons and stirring implements.

Many parts of the fan palm were eaten as food. Indians would sometimes cut out and consume the growing tip of palms. The pith of the crown, a food of last resort, was boiled before being eaten. At times young leaf bases were also consumed.

Without question the most important food resource was the palm fruit. In early fall healthy trees produced ten or more fruit stalks per tree with forty pounds of pea-sized fruits per stalk. In wet years, the harvest might reach 400,000 fruits, totaling 400 pounds per tree. The stalks hung downward but out of human reach. Harvesting was accomplished with a long willow pole, notched at one end. A quick twist broke the stalk and brought the fruit cluster to the ground.

Palm fruit was often eaten fresh, and the small hard seeds were spit out. Indian women sometimes sun-dried the fruit and stored it in large jars. Later the entire fruit would be ground into flour in bedrock mortars after they had been softened by soaking in water. The resultant mush was eaten. Tea was also made, a possible by-product of soaking the fruit in preparation for grinding.

The fan palm is found from Death Valley National Park south into Baja California and east into extreme southern Nevada and western Arizona. In elevation it ranges from below sea level near California's Salton Sea to nearly 4,000 feet in Joshua Tree National Park. It is only found at springs, where water is at or near the surface. The green crown and dead, fan-shaped leaves hanging against the brown trunk distinguish the desert fan palm from all other plants.

Desert Cahuilla house with palm fronds covering walls and roof.

Desert Fan Palm Oasis,
Indian Canyons Tribal Park,
Palm Springs, California.

DESERT WILLOW

(Chilopsis linearis)

The desert willow is not a true willow. It is a member of the Bignonia family, a family that includes a number of well-known ornamentals including Jacaranda and Catalpa. The common name is derived from the long, slender, willow-like leaves. When not in flower, a botanical novice can easily mistake a desert willow for a true willow.

Known to botanists as *Chilopsis linearis*, the desert willow is a large shrub reaching twenty feet in height and confined to usually dry, desert water courses. It is deciduous and the pencil-wide, light-green leaves are dropped each fall. In July the pink to purple flowers mature into slender, seven-inch-long pods. Presence of desert willow indicates groundwater is close to the surface for at least part of the year.

Prior to contact with Europeans in the seventeenth century, the desert willow was important to Native Americans living in the Mojave, Sonoran and Chihuahuan deserts of North America. The wood of the desert willow was the most important part of the plant. The pliable *Chilopsis* branches can be bent nearly in half without breaking or cracking. Though not particularly heavy, they are very strong and highly resistant to decay. For these reasons desert willow wood was important as a construction material for Indian houses. Because of its flexibility, it could be used in rectangular as well as domed structures both as supporting posts and beams.

Many tribes constructed enormous, basket-like structures called *granaries* that would be used to hold mesquite pods and other foods collected in large quantities. Granaries were made by weaving branches around each other and around support poles situated at right angles to the woven branches. Desert willow branches were considered excellent for this purpose, sometimes to the exclusion of all other woody plants.

Blossoms and buds of Desert Willow,
Valley of Fire State Park, Nevada.

Long, straight branches were used as poles to knock fruit from plants that could not be reached by hand. Some Indian cultural groups also made bows from the branches. Forked branches were used to hold round-bottomed ceramic jars and pots. Occasionally the bark was removed and pounded and stretched to make nets and clothing.

Although the flowers and seedpods were sometimes eaten, they were not preferred as food. When dried, however, they made a weak but pleasant-tasting tea. This same liquid was often used as a hot poultice.

Desert willow in bloom, Algodones Dunes, Sonoran Desert, California.

Strong but flexible Desert Willow branches were often used to frame Indian shelters. Photograph taken in the late 1800s courtesy of the Smithsonian Institution.

Fourwing Saltbush in fruit, Wupatki National Monument, Arizona.

FOURWING SALTBUSH
(*Atriplex canescens*)

There are fifteen species of saltbush found in the North American deserts. The genus is named for its tolerance of high soil salinity. In areas where soil salts accumulate because of poor drainage, such as on valley floors and basins, salt bushes thrive. In some areas, they may be the dominant shrub. Of the fifteen species the fourwing saltbush, *Atriplex canescens*, is most abundant and widespread.

The fourwing saltbush is one of the few shrubs that is more appealing in fruit than in flower. Its tiny, wind-pollinated blossoms attract little attention. The fingernail-sized fruits, however, appear in fall and cascade over the plant in massive, yellow-green clusters sometimes completely covering the plant. Each fruit in the cluster has four large *wings* from which the common name is derived. Only half of the saltbushes produce fruit as the species is usually dioecious, with both male (pollen producing) and female (fruit producing) plants.

Nearly every Native American tribe in the Southwest utilized the fourwing saltbush as a food resource. Seeds were knocked out of hanging fruits with a wooden beater and into large, flat baskets. Some Indians then parched the seeds but most ground them up into a meal without parching. The resultant flour was quite nutritious with a protein content exceeding 10%.

Not only were seeds utilized, but leaves and stem tips of the saltbush had value as well. Both contained salt that could easily be detected by taste. For this reason, they were mixed whole or ground in a variety of food preparations, such as mush or stew, to add a pleasant salty taste. Readers today can taste the salt in a few seconds just by chewing the leaves. The Hopi burned these same plant parts and used the ashes as a kind of baking powder.

The fourwing saltbush was used for its medicinal properties as well as food value. The Zuni relieved pain and irritation of insect stings by grinding flowers and roots with saliva to make salve to spread over an inflicted area. Chewing the leaves was said to sooth an upset stomach.

Buffalo Gourd, Cucurbita foetidissima,
Carlsbad Caverns National Park, New Mexico.

GOURD
(Genus *Cucurbita*)

Gourds represent some of the desert's most striking plants. Their large yellow-to-orange flowers, enormous fruits, and extensive creeping vines make them a conspicuous part of the spring and summer flora.

Six species occur in the North American Desert with at least one species occurring in each of the four desert subdivisions. Worldwide there are about thirty species confined to the warmer parts of North and South America. Gourds belong in the genus Cucurbita, a genus that includes domestic squashes and pumpkins.

Today, their colorful names (such as buffalo gourd and coyote melon) along with a striking appearance, capture human attention. Prior to European contact, it was their usefulness that made them important to desert Indians. Depending upon the species, gourds could provide food, medicine, musical instruments, vessels, and perhaps most importantly, soap.

All parts of the gourd contain saponin, a compound useful as a cleansing agent. The root contains the greatest concentration of the compound and was cut into pieces and used like soap cakes. Alternatively, the root pieces might be crushed to make a kind of liquid cleanser.

The Pueblo Indians of the Great Basin Desert obtained oil from the seeds and used it in cooking. Oil comprises approximately thirty percent of the weight of each seed with an even higher protein content. To secure the seeds as food, dried fruits were broken apart and the seeds separated by hand. The seeds were then ground up and mixed with water to form an edible mush.

One gourd species produced a fruit that could be cooked and eaten in its entirety. The pulp, however, contains chemicals called cucurbitacins that taste very bitter and make most fruits unpleasant to consume. For this reason gourd species were not eaten by most cultural groups.

Many parts of the plant were used to treat pain and sickness. The pulp of the green fruit was mixed with soap to form a salve that was spread on skin ulcers and sores to prevent infection and promote healing. Seeds ground into a powder were spread on small, open wounds for the same purpose. A concoction made from gourd roots was placed on larger wounds infested with maggots. If determined that expelling the contents of the stomach or bowels would benefit an ill person, a liquid made from boiled gourd root was given.

The dried fruits were often hollowed out and used as vessels to carry foodstuffs or water. Sometimes the hollow fruit was used as a ladle or converted into a rattle used in celebrations and ceremonies.

Coyote melon, Cucurbita palmata, *Mojave National Preserve, California.*

Bedrock mortar in which gourd, mesquite and many other plant seeds were ground, Indian Canyons Tribal Park, California.

JIMSON WEED
(Genus *Datura*)

Jimson weed is one of the desert's most recognizable plants. It is visually distinctive with broad green leaves, large white flowers, and spine-covered fruits. It also thrives in areas surrounding towns and villages where soil and vegetation are often disturbed by human activities as well as fires and floods.

Jimson weed is one of our most toxic plants. The lives of many children and careless adults have been lost after its leaves, stems, or fruits have been ingested. It is a powerful hallucinogen that was used for centuries by Indian religious leaders (called shamans) skilled in its preparation. All parts of the plant contain the chemicals responsible for toxicity and hallucinogenic effects. Depending upon the purpose of the shaman, the leaves, roots, fruits and nectar from its flowers might be used individually. (Be warned, modern-day experimenters risk their lives by swallowing any part of this plant.)

A shaman ground the leaves in water to make a drink that he consumed in small quantities. Visions received during a hallucinogenic episode gave the shaman special knowledge and power that was shared with other village members. In some tribes the shaman would prepare a similar potion for boys at puberty. The visions, while under the influence of the drug, would speak of the boy's future and predict his role as an adult in tribal society.

There were many other uses of Jimson weed. A paste made from the leaves and stems was applied to broken bones and swollen joints to reduce or eliminate pain. Inhalation of fumes given off by burning or boiling the leaves was effective in relieving respiratory ailments. Indian women were sometimes given Jimson weed seeds to prevent miscarriages. It has also been reported that the Navajo would grind the entire fruit, mix the seeds and pulp with special clay, and then consume the concoction as a food. More recently, scientists have discovered that Jimson weed contains vegetable proteins referred to as lectins. These are known to destroy malignant tumor cells.

Jimson Weed, Datura wrightii,
Red Rock Canyon State Park, California.

JOJOBA

(Simmondsia chinensis)

Jojoba is one of the few Southwest plants that has been cultivated by modern farmers. The jojoba fruit contains a remarkable oil that accounts for 50% of its weight. Unlike petroleum products, jojoba oil needs very little refining and maintains a constant viscosity under extreme temperatures. It is ideal for lubricating high-speed machinery.

For decades the only source of oil with similar properties was produced by sperm whales. By 1970, commercial whaling had driven the whales to the brink of extinction and an intensive search began for a substitute oil. The search eventually led to the jojoba. By 1980, numerous jojoba farms had begun to produce the fruits in quantity. Today, commercially produced jojoba oil has replaced whale oil in nearly all applications. Without a need for sperm whale oil nearly every nation is willing to honor the hunting ban.

Indians of the Southwest were well aware of the oil contained within the fruits of the jojoba. A shampoo was made by grinding up the fruits and applying the concoction to the hair. Sores or skin problems on the head were treated with jojoba oil that was prepared by cooking the fruits in hot ashes and then crushing them on a flat stone called a metate. The salve resulting from this process was spread over the affected area of the scalp. Soreness of the eyes was also treated with jojoba oil. The seeds were ground, put into a straining cloth with the oil, then squeezed out of the cloth and dropped into the patient's eyes.

Jojoba seeds were eaten but not thought to be a particularly nutritious food. The Indians knew (and scientists later explained) that the oil in the jojoba fruits was really an indigestible wax. Half of the fruit offered nothing in the way of nutrition, but as a supplemental food, the bitter-tasting fruits would be eaten fresh or roasted to reveal a pleasant nutty flavor. Grinding up the beans into a powder made a coffee-like drink when mixed with hot water.

Male jojoba plant in bloom,
Sabino Canyon Recreation Area,
Coronado National Forest, Tucson, Arizona.

Two medicinal uses of jojoba have been reported. Chewing raw green seeds was said to eliminate the pain of a sore throat. Indian informants have stated that if a pregnant woman drank strong, cold mixtures of this liquid near the time of birth she would have an easier delivery.

Jojoba is an evergreen shrub with dull, green, leathery leaves. The dark brown, fingernail-sized fruits appear on female plants from May to July. It is found on well-drained soils below 5,000 feet in elevation throughout the Mojave and Sonoran deserts.

Unripe jojoba fruits, Lake Mead National Recreation Area, Nevada.

*Chemehuevi girls preparing food. Note the cottonwood (*Populus fremontii*) branches used to make the frame and the arrow weed (*Pluchea sericea*) stems that fill the walls of the dwelling. Photograph courtesy of the University of Southern California Library.*

JUNIPER
(Genus *Juniperus*)

Junipers are one of the most widespread plant groups in the Southwest. Depending upon the plant taxonomist with whom you speak, there are from nine to twelve species within the boundaries of the North American desert region and about sixty species scattered across the Northern Hemisphere. Though junipers are found in each of the four desert regions in North America, it is the Great Basin Desert and semiarid regions of the West where they may be the dominant plant in both numbers and mass.

Junipers are found at intermediate to high elevations. Occasionally they may be encountered below 2,000 feet on north-facing hillsides or in the shelter of canyons. In past times, most Indian villages were not more than a one day walk from one or more juniper plants.

To Indians of the Southwest, junipers were a very important plant resource because, like the yuccas and agaves, they could be utilized in a variety of ways: as food, seasoning, medicine, tools, firewood, and structural material for houses. As demonstration of junipers' importance, many Indian groups practiced active management by limiting the harvest from individual plants, protecting them from fire, and keeping herbivorous animals away.

In fall, junipers produce large numbers of bluish cones that resemble small berries. In the past, these were harvested as a food resource by nearly every tribe that came in contact with the plants. The Havasuapi of the Grand Canyon broke off berry-laden branches and beat them against blankets spread on the ground. The beating knocked the berries onto the blanket. The Kawaiisu of the Mojave Desert knocked the berries into baskets or picked them up off the ground. Most of the berries would be dried in the sun and then stored for later use. Occasionally the berries might be eaten raw, but normally they were ground into a meal, mixed with water to form mush or pressed by

Utah Juniper, Juniperus osteosperma,
Red Rock Canyon National Recreation Area, Nevada.

hand into cakes that would be consumed later. A variation of this technique was used to make a drink by pounding the berries into pulp and placing the mass in water. The seeds sank to the bottom and the pulp was discarded. The remaining liquid was served as a beverage.

Many Indian tribes believed that relief from a wide assortment of ailments could be obtained from the medicinal qualities of the juniper. That is why some cultural groups routinely carried ground leaves in a pouch attached to a waistband. Several Chihuahuan Desert groups ingested the crushed leaves as a tea to relieve general body pain, stomach ache, or sore throat. A salve might also be made with the leaves to lessen joint pain. The Pima Indians of Arizona concocted a drink from green branches to relieve the symptoms of a cold and inhaled the smoke emanating from burning wood to relieve headaches. The Navaho used extracts from the juniper as a remedy for nausea, acne, insect stings and even post-partum pain.

Juniper Berries
Joshua Tree National Park, California.

The bark of the juniper also had utility. It could be pounded into long fibers and twisted into rope or coiled to a make a *slow match*. In the latter instance, one end of the coil would be lit and kept smoldering for hours, making it easier to start new cooking fires. The bark was also used as tinder when rubbing pieces of wood together to create a fire. Finally, bark was used to fill the seams between logs in house construction as well as stoppers for basket water bottles.

The dead, standing trunks of large junipers were highly prized for the bow-making qualities. Large slivers of trunk (called staves) were peeled off by using a stone chisel hammered at an angle into the trunk. Using this technique from both the top and the bottom, the raw wood for a three to four-foot-long bow could be obtained.

MESQUITE
(Genus *Prosopis*)

Without question mesquite was the most important food plant for Native Americans living in the Sonoran, Chihuahuan and Mojave deserts. With deep roots that often reach down to the water table, mesquite produces some fruit even in the driest of years. So reliable is this food resource that, in past times, village sites were usually selected because of mesquite proximity.

In good years a large mesquite produces over twenty pounds of fruit that can easily be collected by hand. An individual fruit of the honey mesquite, *Prosopis glandulosa*, can reach seven inches in length and form a flat pod containing several seeds or *beans*. The pods hang in large clusters and their whose combined weight can bend a branch to the ground. As the fruit dries and falls, the pods pile up to form a tan carpet beneath the shrub.

Fruits ripen in summer and early fall and prior to European contact were collected and stored in large basket granaries for use in winter. Entire fruits, including the enclosed seeds, were crushed in rock or wooden mortars. The resulting meal was placed in an earthen bowl and thoroughly mixed with water. The resulting mush was eaten or made into cakes and dried. The cakes were an ideal food for transport during seasonal migrations or hunting trips.

Although the pods were the most important resource, all parts of the mesquite were used to some extent. The flowers were collected in the spring, roasted, and then pressed into a ball for eating. A tea was made by boiling the blossoms in water. A tea was also made from the leaves that was said to inhibit diarrhea.

Concoctions made from the leaves and twigs were used as a disinfectant on cuts and abrasions. Conjunctivitis of any type was treated by washing the eyes with a rinse made from the pods. The sap was used as an adhesive. The trunk could be hollowed out at the top and used as a mortar for grinding. Mesquite branches were considered to make superior bows. All woody parts of the plant made excellent firewood. Mesquite charcoal is sold today because of the pleasant flavor it adds to meat.

The mesquite is a large, spreading shrub (rarely a tree) with long, compound leaves made up of tiny leaflets and long thorns on the branches. Depending upon the species, the fuzzy, pale yellow flowers mature into flat or tightly coiled fruits.

Mesquite is found below 5,000 feet around springs and valley bottoms wherever water is at or near the surface. It is confined to the relatively warm Sonoran, Mojave and Chihuahuan deserts and absent from the colder Great Basin Desert.

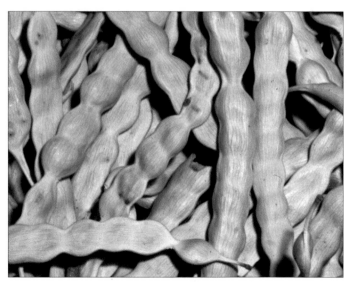

Mesquite pods (fruits)

Honey Mesquite, Prosopis glandulosa, *in bloom,*
Death Valley National Park, California.

Mormon Tea
(Genus *Ephedra*)

*Bunches of these twigs are almost universally to be
found tucked among the thatching of every jacal (hut)
or packed away in basket or olla.*
— David Prescott Barrows, 1900

All tribes in the Southwest had access to, and drank, Mormon tea. As the common name suggests, a hot drink was made from the shrub and was considered both refreshing and therapeutic.

Many persons, both Indian and non-Indian, still use stems to make tea. The process is essentially the same that was used hundreds, probably thousands of years ago. Stems are cut from a shrub (usually in late summer) and can be used immediately or stored almost indefinitely. A handful are placed in a bowl of boiling water and removed from the heat source to allow the liquid to steep for twenty minutes. Adding more stems, or increasing the brewing time, makes a stronger tea.

Indians drank the tea to cure canker sores in the mouth, eliminate kidney ailments, purify the blood, relieve cold symptoms, eliminate ulcers, and relieve stomach disorders. Conversely, most Indians said drinking too much of the tea caused temporary bowel disorders, a reality sometimes mentioned by modern-day Mormon tea aficionados.

Boiling, instead of brewing, the stems revealed additional qualities. The Navajo boiled stems of *Ephedra viridis* to make a dye. Pima Indians boiled the stems to make a drink considered a remedy for intestinal ailments as well as syphilis and gonorrhea.

Occasionally, dried stems or roots were ground to powder and applied to open sores. For burns, the powder was moistened and used as a poultice. It is also known that an infusion prepared from the tiny leaves and blossoms was used to flush out the kidneys.

Mormon Tea, Ephedra californica, *in bloom,
Anza-Borrego Desert State Park, California.*

Mormon tea was valuable as a food resource for some tribes. The Panamint Indians collected the large black seeds and roasted them prior to consumption. Occasionally, they would grind the seeds to make mush or bake a bitter-tasting bread. Chewing the raw stems also increased salivation as a temporary relief from thirst.

Mormon tea is a densely branched shrub with yellow-green to blue-green stems depending upon the species. There are no obvious leaves and the flowers are small and often go unnoticed. Plants are found on coarse-soiled alluvial plains and hillsides below 8,000 feet in elevation from the southern Great Basin Desert of Nevada, through the Mojave and Sonoran deserts into the Chihuahuan Desert of west Texas.

Mormon tea, Ephedra viridis, *in bloom,*
Red Rock Canyon National Conservation Area, Las Vegas, Nevada.

Indian woman beating seeds into a tray basket.

OCOTILLO
(*Fouquieria splendens*)

Every part of the ocotillo was used by Native Americans. Apache Indians ground the roots into a powder and mixed it with warm water to make a soothing, fatigue-relieving bath. A root tea was used to reduce the moist coughing of elderly people. Root powder was also applied to swollen joints and contusions to reduce swelling.

Ignaz Pfefferkorn, an early Spanish traveler, related how ocotillo was used to reduce swelling and pain: *"A Spaniard who, with some Indians, accompanied me on a journey, fell with his horse so his right leg lay under the animal. Because of the weight lying upon it, the leg was crushed and swollen to such a size . . . that in order to lay it bare, the boot and stocking had to be cut open . . . an Indian . . . lighted a fire immediately, cut off some twigs from the ocotillo and after peeling these, roasted the remainder for a short time in hot ashes. Then he pressed out the juice on a cloth and bound the leg with it. This treatment he repeated several times and in two hours' time the swelling was gone and the Spaniard was without the least pain."*

Ocotillo branches made excellent firewood. Branches were also used to make a living fence by shoving them into the ground side by side and watering them every few days. The branches would soon take root and, aided by their thorns, were effective barriers against rabbits trying to invade Indian gardens.

Most Indian groups collected the spring-appearing red blossoms and mixed them with water to produce a tasty drink. After the blossoms wilted, seeds were collected, parched, and ground into flour. The flour could be made into mush by mixing it with water or formed into cakes by allowing the mush to dry. Ocotillo seeds were nutritious with a 29% protein content.

The ocotillo is found on coarse-soiled alluvial plains and hillsides from the Sonoran to the Chihuahuan deserts of western Texas. It ranges in elevation from below sea level near California's Salton Sea to 4,600 feet in Arizona and Texas.

Ocotillos after summer rain,
Big Bend National Park, Texas.

ORGAN PIPE CACTUS
(Stenocereus thurberi)

The organ pipe cactus produces a flavorful fruit. Many people, including Tohono O'odham Indians, believe organ pipe fruit—with a taste reminiscent of watermelon—is better tasting than saguaro fruit. Indians have harvested it for centuries and some still gather it today.

Fruit ripens in summer and fall. Usually women were responsible for collecting the tennis ball-sized spheres. Fruit grows near the top of the stems and was skewered with a pole that had a small, sharp stick fastened to its tip. After the spines had been removed, the fruit was eaten (the skin is edible) or peeled, sliced and dried for storage. Dried fruit was moistened with water and then eaten raw or cooked. Fruit pulp could be mixed with water to make a sweet syrup. The syrup was poured into ceramic pots called *ollas*. The pots were then sealed to allow the mixture to ferment into wine.

Organ pipe cactus fruits are packed with seeds. Although Indians of southern Arizona and Sonora did not utilize them, presumably because the seeds were too small, at least some of the Indians of Baja California collected and ground them into meal. The technique used for separating the seeds from the fruit was unusual. According to a description written in 1740 by Father Consag, Indians spent several weeks in one locality collecting and consuming organ pipe fruits. They made it a point to defecate in selected spots so they could return and collect their dry feces the following year. Feces were ground by hand to winnow out undigested organ pipe seeds. They were then toasted, ground on metates and eaten. This "second harvest," as it was called, was totally objectionable to early missionaries but was efficient in tapping a source of food that was otherwise difficult to utilize.

Organ pipe cactus grows to 24 feet in height and is characterized by numerous erect, unbranched, and spine-covered stems. It is found on coarse soils below 3,000 feet in elevation in and around Organ Pipe Cactus National Monument and south into Sonora and Baja California.

PINYON
(Genus *Pinus*)

Pinyon pines are one of the most widespread plant groups in the Southwest covering at least 75,000 square miles of plateau, hillside, and mountain terrain. Although they are found in each of the four desert regions in North America, it is the Great Basin Desert and semiarid regions of the West where they may be the dominant plant in both numbers and mass. Pinyons are found at intermediate to high elevations, often growing in close association with junipers. In past times, most Indian villages were not more than one or two day's walk from stands of these important trees.

Pinyon pines are a subgroup of pine trees all very closely related and all with the same general appearance. Each is short of stature, as pine trees go, with the very tallest not even reaching fifty feet and most individuals less than thirty-five feet in height. Often the trees are asymmetrical and gnarly, reflecting the erratic and meager precipitation they receive. The needles are short and born in clusters of from one to five depending upon the species. The cones, which bear the nuts, are small, rarely with a diameter exceeding three inches. The cones and tasty nuts ripen in the fall and, in some localities, are harvested commercially, packaged, and sent to grocery stores.

In past times, native desert people migrated up into the high mountains in late summer or fall to harvest nuts. The practice would take several weeks and an entire family would participate. If the cones had already opened, the seeds would be knocked out with a long pole. If the cones were still closed, whole cones would be knocked from the tree and then placed on a fire causing them to open and release the nuts. The nuts themselves would be roasted and then cracked to remove the shells. Occasionally the stick-mound nests of woodrats would be sifted by Indians to locate pinyon nuts harvested by the rodent.

Harvesting pinyon nuts was a rewarding endeavor. It has been said that a husband and wife with two children could harvest more than

Colorado Pinyon, Pinus edulis,
Grand Canyon National Park, Arizona.

200 pounds of nuts in a single day. (The shells of the nuts are waste and account for about forty percent of the harvest. That leaves a total useable food weight of 120 pounds from a 200 pound harvest.)

Pinyon expert Ronald Lanner has found that a pound of shelled pinyon nuts yields approximately 2,800 calories. That translates into a harvest of 336,000 calories per day. If we assume that each member of the family requires 2,000 calories per day to live then a single day's harvest of pinyon nuts would provide enough food for the entire family for six weeks!

Although an Indian family would not have consumed only pinyon nuts for six weeks, the nuts are very nourishing. The shelled nuts average 15 percent protein, a fat content usually exceeding 20 percent, and a carbohydrate content of at least 14 percent. There are also important amounts of iron, vitamin A, thiamine, riboflavin and niacin.

Pinyon with cones,
Great Basin National Park, Nevada.

RUSH
(Genus *Juncus*)

One of the most common plants found at desert seeps, springs and streams is rush. Technically referred to as *Juncus* by botanists, this family of plants has a worldwide distribution. Dozens of species occur within the boundaries of the North American Desert (though some species are introduced from distant lands). It is not uncommon for more than one species to occur at a single spring with individual species forming dense patches in saturated soils.

The most conspicuous rush species consist of numerous green, erect, unbranching stems reaching from one to four feet in height. Stems may develop from rhizomes or from a root crown, depending upon the species. The stem tip of some species forms a sharp spine. Inconspicuous flowers are produced from spring to early fall and appear near stem tips.

Though rushes were utilized in several ways by Native Americans, basket manufacturing was the paramount use. By the time European settlers arrived in the American Southwest there was not a single Indian group that did not utilize baskets made, at least in part, of *Juncus*. Rush baskets were used as temporary containers, long-term storage vessels, mixing bowls for food and medicine, elements in ceremonies, gifts, medium of exchange (as an item of trade), and hats. Baskets were strong but light in weight, surprisingly durable, made in a variety of sizes and shapes (some were larger than a beach ball), and often designed to be aesthetically pleasing. By the early 20th century baskets were also made for tourists. Such baskets often incorporated elaborate patterns and designs made of *Juncus*. Today these same baskets have found their way into museum collections around the world and are sometimes appraised at thousands of dollars.

Historically, baskets were made by women and could take from days to months of intermittent sewing to complete. Several plants were used to make a coiled basket (the dominant style of basket construction at the time of European settlement in the Southwest). *Yucca* fibers were typically used to start the basket and deer grass (Genus *Muhlenbergia*) or *Juncus* used to form what is called the "rod." *Juncus* was one of the favored sewing materials to wrap around the rod and is, therefore, the part of a coiled basket that one actually sees.

The late anthropologist David Prescott Barrows described how *Juncus* was readied for basket construction (words in parentheses are author's):

> It (Juncus) *grows abundantly in cienaga or in damp soil. The scape (flower stalk) and leaves are two to four feet high, or more, stout and pungent. A supply of these tough scapes is gathered by the basket maker and cut off at a suitable length. She then takes a rush by one end and with her teeth splits it into three equal portions, carefully separating the entire length of the piece. Each scape thus furnishes three withes. This reed is near its base, of a deep red, lightening in color upwards, passing through several shades of light brown, and ending at the top in a brownish yellow. Thus this bulrush* (Juncus)*, in its natural state, furnishes a variety of colors.*

Though dyes were often used for color in basket making, the subdued browns, oranges and yellows of *Juncus* stems were both natural and unique. Some of the most beautiful coiled baskets in existence have patterns created from naturally colored *Juncus* stems.

Rushes also provided diversity to the Indian diet. New, tender stems were occasionally collected and eaten without preparation. The Paiute of California's Owens Valley were known to harvest the seeds in the fall. The seeds were usually mixed with other seeds and ground into flour. It can be assumed that many other Indian groups also harvested *Juncus* seeds.

Spiny Rush, Juncus acutus, *Indian Canyons Tribal Park, Palm Springs, California.*

SAGEBRUSH
(*Artemisia tridentata*)

Many plants are called sagebrush, but *big sagebrush* is the most widespread covering much of the western United States. Just as the creosote bush is the dominant shrub of the three warm deserts; big sagebrush is the dominant shrub of the cooler Great Basin Desert.

With the exception of roots, Native Americans used all parts of the plant. The bitter leaves are antimicrobial in nature and have medicinal value. In historic times leaves were soaked in water to make an extremely bitter tea used as a tonic to prevent illness. Leaves were also used to cleanse the hair and eyes, as an antiseptic for wounds and, when taken internally, a cure for colds and upset stomachs.

A powder was made with dried and ground leaves, serving as a remedy for moist skin rashes and chafing. Breathing the fumes from burning or boiling the leaves was considered purifying and helpful in keeping the respiratory tract clear. Fume breathing was done in the home, in the sweathouse (a sauna) or as part of religious ceremonies.

The strong-scented leaves and stems were sometimes laid over perishable foods, such as berries and tubers, to preserve them. Leaves were also placed around seed caches to deter insect and rodent attacks. They were often used as construction and insulating material for dwellings.

Big sagebrush flowers first appear in July. Certain tribes collected the pollen for use in religious ceremonies. The pollinated flowers would turn to seed beginning in September. The Paiute Indians of Nevada gathered the seeds in large quantities, parched them and ground them into meal. A nutritious mush was made with the addition of water.

Sagebrush branches and trunk were often burned because of the smoke's pleasant fragrance. Occasionally, the bark would be stripped off and peeled or pounded into fibers for use in basket construction.

Big sagebrush is identified by its aromatic foliage. Leaves are narrow and gray-green in color. Bark is gray and hangs in shreds from branches.

Big Sagebrush, Artemisia tridentata,
Mono Basin National Forest Scenic Area, California.

SAGUARO
(*Carnegiea gigantea*)

The giant saguaro cactus was so important to the O'odham Indians of Arizona that the harvest of its fruit marked the beginning of the new year. In June and early July, Indian families camped in saguaro forests and initiated the harvest.

Since saguaros are trees that reach fifty feet in height, and because the plum-size fruits develop at the top of the spiny branches and trunk, the fruits cannot be picked by hand but must be dislodged with a tool. The Tohono O'odham did this by striking the fruits with a long wooden pole made from the rib of a dead saguaro. Usually a small stick was attached to the tip of the pole which functioned as a hook to loosen the fruit. Once on the ground, the fruits were collected by hand.

Before carrying the fruit back to camp, the red inner pulp was scooped out and the skin discarded. A portion of the pulp was eaten fresh but most of it was placed into a large olla and soaked in water to loosen the small, black seeds. The seeds were strained off and the pulp cooked. The water was boiled away leaving a thick syrup in the olla. After the syrup cooled it was placed in ceramic vessels and sealed with mud to preserve it for later use as a sweetener with meals. Allowed to ferment, it became saguaro wine.

After the saguaro harvest, an important ceremony took place which included dancing, singing and drinking of the intoxicating wine. The final preparation of the wine involved pouring water and the saguaro syrup into watertight baskets. The water and syrup were mixed and then poured into ollas. The mixture was allowed to ferment for approximately four days before being consumed at the harvest celebration. The wine would spoil within twenty-four hours, so there was some attempt by the men to consume all of it.

Seeds of the saguaro were ground with water to make a gruel used to make bread. In more recent times, the ground seeds were mixed with cholla buds and wheat flour to induce milk production in wet nurses.

Saguaro cacti,
Organ Pipe Cactus National Monument.

Tobacco
(Genus *Nicotiana*)

Most cultural groups considered tobacco a sacred plant and used it in nearly every ceremony and ritual. Smoking tobacco helped the mind drive away negative spiritual visions, enhance thoughts of increased land productivity, or help connect to the spiritual world. If a man were to embark upon a long journey, a shaman might blow tobacco smoke in his direction of travel to ward off danger and hardship.

Smoking was done with a pipe made of stone, clay or plant stem. Tobacco was prepared for smoking by drying the leaves, grinding them up, and mixing the tobacco with other ground up plants.

The importance of tobacco is reflected in its widespread cultivation. Tribes that practiced agriculture raised tobacco. In many cases tribes that did not raise any food crops still actively cultivated it. Seeds were planted, weeding practiced, and vegetation burned off to ready the ground for tobacco planting. Cultivation was usually a special, even secret affair. The Tohono O'odam of the Sonoran Desert sowed seeds in hidden fields to bring out the tobacco's special qualities.

Each of the numerous species of tobacco contains alkaloids that can be highly toxic, even deadly. Thus, its use was confined to shamans and adults having a thorough knowledge of its properties. These persons used tobacco as a medicinal agent for a wide variety of ailments. Swelling of the joints from rheumatism or injury was said to be reduced by applying tobacco poultices. Such poultices could also be applied to skin infections. Placed on the gums, tobacco concoctions could alleviate toothache. Shamans might also chew the leaves and spread the paste over a rattlesnake bite. Among many tribes, smoking tobacco was thought to cure colds. Mixed with water, a tobacco drink could induce vomiting. Shamans were known to remedy an earache by blowing tobacco smoke into the afflicted person's ear.

At least one species of tobacco can be found in each of the four North American deserts. Tobacco plants generally occur on coarse soils and are characterized by undivided leaves, white to yellow flowers and tubular corollas.

Desert Tobacco, Nicotiana trigonophylla,
Santa Rosa and San Jacinto Mountains National Monument.

YUCCA
(Genus *Yucca*)

Yuccas were revered by Native Americans because they were an excellent source of food, fiber and soap. Not only did yuccas have practical applications, they were used for ceremonial purposes as well.

Fifteen species of yucca exist within the desert areas of the United States. With so many kinds of yucca, Indians found at least one species in close proximity to most villages.

Soap was one of the yucca's most important products. The roots contain saponin, a detergent-like compound. Pounding the roots in water produces copious suds. Indians used these suds to wash their hair and clothes, and for ritual cleansing in ceremonies. Among the Hopi, the head of a child was washed with yucca suds on the twentieth day after birth, first by the paternal grandmother and then by each member of the father's family. Yavapai warriors, returning from battle, purified themselves by taking yucca baths.

As a fiber-producing plant, the yucca was without parallel, particularly the Mojave yucca (*Yucca schidigera*). Fiber was prepared by soaking the leaves in water, placing them on a flat rock and pounding away the softer tissues with a wooden club. What remained were tough white filaments that could be twisted together to form threads. Yucca threads were used to make sandals, rope, mats, clothing elements, nets, and mattresses. Yucca fibers were also used in baskets. In the initial stages of construction, pliable but strong yucca fibers were incorporated into the first few coils at the bottom of the basket. Red and brown designs were often made by weaving in strands of the inner fibers of Joshua tree (*Yucca brevifolia*) roots.

Flower stalks, blossoms and seeds of all yucca species were consumed. Fruits of the banana yucca (*Yucca baccata),* were particularly relished and eaten raw, baked, boiled, dried or ground into meal.

Soaptree Yucca (Yucca elata) *in bloom,*
Big Bend National Park, Texas.

Though fruits were eaten in their entirety after cooking, the skin and seeds were often discarded. The remaining pulp was crushed into a paste and sun-dried for several days, then kneaded into cakes that could be stored for winter use.

Yuccas are characterized by long spine-tipped leaves, white to pale yellow blossoms and large, massive flower clusters.

Indian sandal made of Yucca fibers,
Museum of the Big Bend, Alpine, Texas.

*Mojave Yucca (*Yucca schidigera*) in foreground,*
*Joshua Tree (*Yucca brevifolia*) in background,*
Joshua Tree National Park, California.

Juan Jose Montoya and his daughter, Ignacia Adelaido Montoya, at Cochiti Pueblo,
November 30, 1880. Ignacia is using a mano to crush plant seeds on a metate.
Photograph by George C. Bennett, Courtesy Museum of New Mexico.

References

Anderson, M. K. 2005. *Tending The Wild.*
University of California Press, Berkeley, California.

Barrows, D. P. 1967. *Ethno-botany of the Cahuilla Indians.*
Malki Museum Press, Banning, California.

Bean, L. J. and K. S. Saubel. 1972. *Temalpakh.*
Malki Museum Press, Banning, California.

Blackburn, T. C. and K. Anderson. 1993. *Before the Wilderness.*
Ballena Press, Menlo Park, California.

Cornett, J. W. 2010. *Desert Palm Oasis: A Comprehensive Guide.*
Nature Trails Press, Palm Springs, California.

Cornett, J. W. 2000. *Saguaro: Questions and Answers.*
Palm Springs Desert Museum, Palm Springs, California.

Curtin, L. S. M. 1947. (Revised and edited by M. Moore, 1997).
Healing herbs of the Upper Rio Grande.
Western Edge Press, Santa Fe, New Mexico.

Curtin, L. S. M. 1949. *By the Prophet of the Earth: Ethnobotany of the Pima.*
University of Arizona Press, Tucson, Arizona.

Dunmire, W. W. and G. D. Tierney. 1997. *Wild Plants and Native Peoples of the Four Corners.* Museum of New Mexico, Santa Fe, New Mexico.

Ebeling, W. 1986. *Handbook of Indian Foods and Fibers of Arid America.*
University of California Press, Berkeley, California.

Felger, R. S. and M. B. Moser. 1985. *People of the Desert and Sea.*
University of Arizona Press, Tucson, Arizona.

Hickman, J. C. (editor). 1993. *The Jepson Manual.*
University of California Press, Berkeley, California.

Hodgson, W. C. 2001. *Food Plants of the Sonoran Desert.*
University of Arizona Press, Tucson, Arizona.

Jaeger, E. C. 1969. *Desert Wild Flowers.*
Stanford University Press, Stanford, California.

Kay, M. A. 1996. *Healing with plants.*
University of Arizona Press, Tucson, Arizona.

Kirk, D. R. 1970. *Wild edible plants.*
Naturegraph Publishers, Healdsburg, California.

Lanner, R. M. 1981. *The Pinyon Pine.*
University of Nevada Press, Reno, Nevada.

Moore, M. 1989. *Medicinal Plants of the Desert and Canyon West.*
Museum of New Mexico Press, Santa Fe, New Mexico.

Nabhan, G. P. 1985. *Gathering the Desert.*
University of Arizona Press, Tucson, Arizona.

Niethammer, C. 1974. *American Indian Food and Lore.*
Macmillan Publishing Company, New York, New York.

Phillips, S. J. and P. W. Comus (editors). 2000. *A Natural History of the Sonoran Desert.* Arizona-Sonora Desert Museum Press, Tucson, Arizona.

Rea, A. M. 1997. *At the Desert's Green Edge.*
University of Arizona Press, Tucson, Arizona.

Rhode, D. 2002. *Native Plants of Southern Nevada: An Ethnobotany.*
University of Utah Press, Salt Lake City, Utah.

Roberts, N. C. 1989. *Baja California Plant Field Guide.*
Natural History Publishing Company, La Jolla, California.

Stewart, J. M. 1993. *Colorado Desert Wildflowers.*
Published by Jon Stewart Photography, Albuquerque, New Mexico.

Stewart, J. M. 1998. *Mojave Desert Wildflowers.*
Published by Jon Stewart Photography, Albuquerque, New Mexico.

Turner, M. W. 2009. *Remarkable Plants of Texas.*
University of Texas Press, Austin, Texas.

Weber, S. A. and P. D. Seaman (editors). 1985. *Havasupai Habitat.*
University of Arizona Press, Tucson, Arizona.

Yetman, D. 2006. *Organ Pipe Cactus.*
University of Arizona Press, Tucson, Arizona.

About the author . . .

James W. Cornett received B.A. and M.S. degrees in biology. His writings on desert Indians include two books—*How Indians Use Desert Plants* and *Indians and Desert Animals*—and articles in scientific journals including Masterkey, the publication of the Southwest Museum. He developed several major exhibitions on desert Indians at the Palm Springs Desert Museum where he was Curator of Natural Science for nearly 30 years.